Judy Collins Anthology

...trust your heart

Amsco Publications
New York/London/Sydney/Cologne

PHOTO CREDITS

Front cover photography by Francesco Scavullo
David Gahr/pages 4 and 7
Ebet Roberts/page 4
Julie Snow/page 4
Suzanne Szasz/page 7
Scott Weiner/Retna Ltd./page 7

All other photographs from the collection of Judy Collins

Arranged and edited by Frank Metis

Copyright © 1988 by Amsco Publications
A Division of Music Sales Corporation, New York, NY.

Order Number: AM 71200
US International Standard Book Number: 0.8256.2533.5
UK International Standard Book Number: 0.7119.1490.7

Exclusive Distributors:
Music Sales Corporation
257 Park Avenue South, New York, NY 10010 USA
Music Sales Limited
8/9 Frith Street, London W1V 5TZ England
Music Sales Pty. Limited
120 Rothschild Street, Rosebery, Sydney, NSW 2018, Australia

Printed in the United States of America by
Vicks Lithograph and Printing Corporation

My Voice Teacher Max Margolies and I

My Sister Holly and I

Judy Collins with Geraldo Rivera
1975 ABC-TV News

Judy Collins with Tom Clancy

Judy Collins with Rona Elliot (of VH-1)
at Farm Aid II.

My Parent's house on 1st ave. in Seattle Washington. (I'm standing at the top of the stairs with my doll and carriage)(age 3)

Me and "Poochie"
1941

Mom, Dad, my brother Michael and me.
Under the tree at 11572 Mississippi Ave. L.A.
1946

At my son Clark's wedding (1987): (L-R) Peter and Sandy Bergen, Louis Nelson, Alyson Taylor, Clark Taylor, me, and Peter Taylor

Me singing with the Rock and Roll band at the Gilded Garter, Central City, Colorado. 1959

Portrait of Judy Collins 1969

Relaxing with Louis Nelson 1987

Judy Collins and Louis Nelson
1987

On Stage

Singing with the guitar 1965

Judy with Joan Baez, producer/friend
Mark Abramson, and David Anville is in
the background. 1966

Judy with Leonard Cohen and the "Young Tradition" Newport, R.I. 1967

Amazing Grace

This song was written by John Newton, an eighteenth-century slave trader. He is reported to have been involved in a shipwreck from which he was saved. Upon regaining his health he wrote "Amazing Grace" and was said to have spent the rest of his life in an effort to abolish the practice of trading slaves. The song has become a multinational, multiracial, and multi-denominational anthem.

Arranged and Adapted by
Judy Collins

Cook With Honey

This little song came to me in the early seventies, in the beginning of the nutritional revolution. It seemed to put into words all the things we were thinking about: good eating, good loving, and good living.

Words and Music by
Valerie Carter

Secret Gardens

Journal writing has been an important part of my life since the mid sixties. I often turn
to my journals when looking for any inspiration for a song. "My grandmother's house is
still there" was the entry I made on returning from Grandmother Byrd's funeral in Seattle
in 1972.

Words and Music by
Judy Collins

Freely, with motion

My grand-moth-er's house is still there, but it is-n't the same. A plain wood-en cot-tage, a patch of brown

Send In The Clowns

This song fused the many diverse aspects of my music into one cohesive line. After I heard it, recorded it, and saw how much of my own musical taste it embodied, I began to understand what Duke Ellington meant when he said, "There are only two kinds of music: good and bad," and categories finally fell away.

Words and Music by
Stephen Sondheim

Running For My Life

There are dreams whose energy to provoke us seems relentless and inevitable, although it is often wise to stand still and let them pass. There are moments when all one can do is move at great speed.

Words and Music by
Judy Collins

Riding the night train, New York to L. A.,
gonna go and get me some sunshine. Clipping along t'ward the Colorado Rockies,

Open The Door (Song For Judith)

My friend Judith Weston's vitality and enthusiasm for life inspired this song.
I wrote it while observing her crochet a rainbow of the world.

Words and Music by
Judy Collins

41

Hard Times For Lovers

Words and Music by
Hugh Prestwood

Mama Mama

Words and Music by
Judy Collins

48

50

2. Wonder if you know just how it feels to be alone,
   Tryin' to raise a bunch of kids on nothin' but love and guts.
   When the day is over I'm about as wrecked as a body can be,
   I got my troubles, but again I need me some kind of lovin',

   Don't know how it happened one more time,
   The money's runnin' out and the other kids are cryin'.
   Somebody tell me I'm not crazy,
   Doin' what I can to raise my babies. *(Chorus)*

3. The doctor down in Lincoln said I'd be all right,
   He said he didn't want to help me but he'd do it just this once.
   Made me feel so bad I couldn't stop the tears from fallin',
   Made me wish he had to pay this kind of price for his lovin'.

   Don't know how it happened one more time,
   The money's runnin' out and the other kids are cryin'.
   Five kids are gonna drive me crazy,
   Lord, I can't have another baby. *(Chorus)*

Born To The Breed

Although this song was written about my own child, the feelings have been experienced by most people I know who have children. The time comes when the chicks leave the nest, and one wishes them everything wonderful in life.

Words and Music by
Judy Collins

I was on-ly nine-teen   The morn-ing you were born,   With your hair fine and red,___   And your

try - in' to get to the sky.

2. Homeward through the streets
   With you in my arms.
   Cold winter mornings
   In a Colorado town.
   I've seen you stumble,
   You've watched me fall,
   You know I've got nothing,
   You know we've got it all.

3. Back in September
   You call me on the phone.
   Ma, you know I love you,
   But I gotta be on my own.
   Comes a time in a boy's life
   When he's got to be a man.
   Please don't try to find me,
   Please try to understand.

4. Now he's playing guitar
   In a rock and roll band,
   Lookin' like a baby,
   Talkin' like a man.
   The life of a guitar man
   Is a hard life to lead,
   What can I tell you,
   You were born to the breed.

5. I've watched you growing
   Through all these years.
   You seen me stumble,
   I've watched your tears.
   Sometimes there was roses,
   Sometimes there was thorns,
   But I know you're gonna make it,
   As sure as you were born.
   (To Coda)

Song For Duke

Duke Ellington's funeral was one of the spiritual stepping stones of my life. His leaving
was poignantly accompanied by the jazz artists of our time. At St. John the Divine's
church, the music of Billy Taylor, Sarah Vaughn, Ella Fitzgerald—and the memory of the
Duke himself—inspired me to write this song.

Words and Music by
Judy Collins

as it has so man-y oth-ers._____ I knew that he had

died that week, af-ter fight-ing death a year or more._____

_____ But I had had a rule be-fore that fun'rals were a waste of

flow-ers._____ But some-thing said I had to go,___

Ché

This song took me five years to write. The images of the power of the Catholic Church, agrarian reform in South America, and the fickle ferocity of the nature of leadership led me to fuse the concept of radical movement and the individual with that of inevitable responsibility.

Words and Music by
Judy Collins

One morn-ing in Bo-liv-i-a, the lead-er of the Par-ti-sans and two of his com-pan-ions___ were forced-to flee the moun-tains for their lives. Through

They on-ly tell you they can show_you, and then to-mor-row they are gone._____

To next strain *Fine*

The gone._____

Moderately, quasi a tempo

smell of oil and in-cense fill the room in this a-do-be

hut where on the ta-ble lies the bod-y of a

Houses

The symbols and poetry in this song came directly from a dream I had which I set to music.
The melody reminds me of my early classical training.

Words and Music by
Judy Collins

You have man-y hous-es,
one for ev-ery sea-son.
Mountains in your win-dows,
vio-lets in your hand.
Through your Eng-lish mead-ows your

When the win-ter finds you, you
fly to where it's sum-mer.
Rooms that face the o-cean,
moon-light on your bed.
Mer-maids swift as dol-phins

73

The Fisherman Song

Words and Music by
Judy Collins

Verse 3.
Way out on the ocean, the big ships hunt for whales;
The Japanese have caught so many that now they hunt for snails.
My fisherman's not greedy, he seems content to live
With the sun and the sand and a net full of fishes when the tide turns.

(Chorus)

Farewell To Tarwathie

Words and Music by
Judy Collins

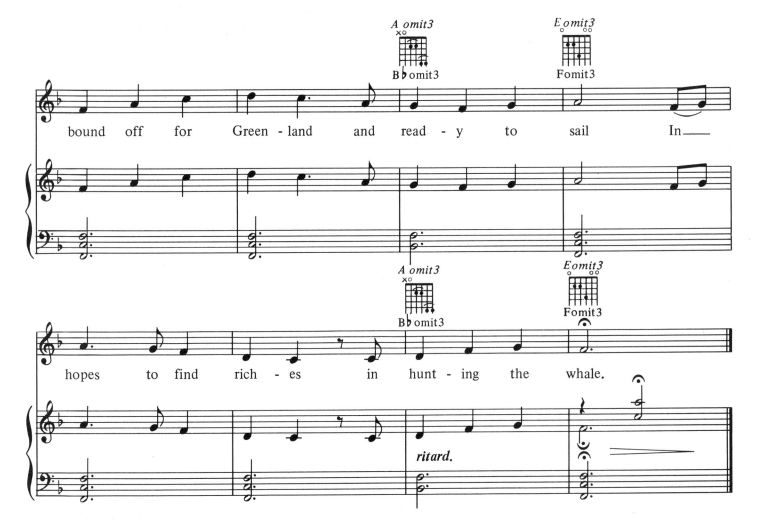

bound off for Green - land and read - y to sail In___

hopes to find rich - es in hunt - ing the whale.

ritard.

2. Farewell to my comrades for a while we must part,
   And like the dear lass who first won my heart,
   The cold coast of Greenland my love will not chill,
   And the longer my absence more loving she'll feel.

3. Our ship is well rigged and she's ready to sail,
   The crew they are anxious to follow the whale
   Where the icebergs do form and the stormy winds blow,
   Where the land and the ocean is covered with snow.

4. The cold coast of Greenland is barren and bare,
   No seed time nor harvest is ever known there.
   And the birds here sing sweetly in mountain and dale,
   But there's no bird in Greenland to sing to the whale.

5. There is no habitation for a man to live there,
   And the King of that country is the fierce Greenland bear.
   And there'll be no temptation to tarry long there,
   With our ship bumper full we will homeward repair.

6. Farewell to Tarwathie, adieu Mormand Hill
   And the dear land of Crimmond, I bid thee farewell.
   We're bound off for Greenland and ready to sail
   In hopes to find riches in hunting the whale.

Marjorie

Adapted and Arranged by
Judy Collins

Marieke

Original Words by Jacques Brel
English Words by Eric Blau
Original Music by Jacques Brel & Gerard Jouannest

Zon - der lief - de, waarm - de lief - de, Weent de zee dé - jà fin - i.____

Zon - der lief - de, waarm - de lief - de, Lijdt het licht, tout est fin - i,____ En

schuurt het zand o - ver mijn land, Mijn plat - te land,____ mijn Vlaan - deren - land.

poco rit.

Moderately bright, in 3, with a lilt

Ay, Ma - rie - ke, Ma - rie - ke, Le ciel fla - mand,
Ay, Ma - rie - ke, Ma - rie - ke, Sur tes vingt ans,

92

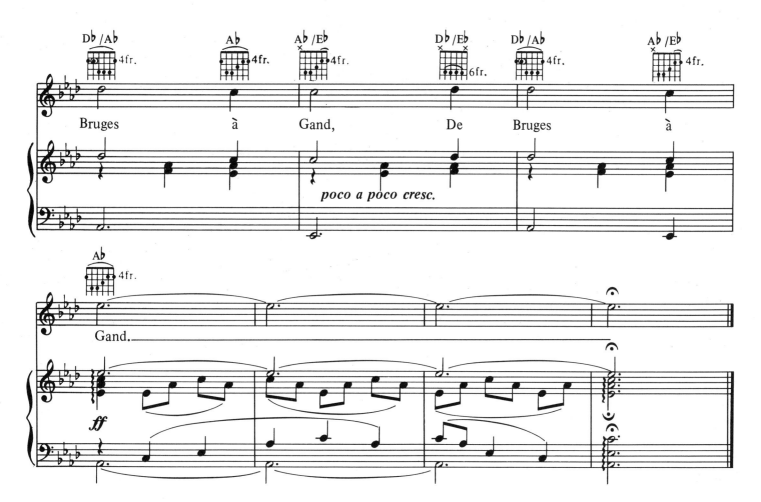

Ay, Marieke, Marieke, I loved you so much
Between the towers of Bruges and Ghent,
Ay, Marieke, Marieke, a long time ago,
Between the towers of Bruges and Ghent.

    Without love, warm love,
    The wind, the dense wind, blows,
    Without love, warm love,
    The sea, the grey sea, sweeps.
    Without love, warm love,
    The light, the dark light, flickers,
    And the ship whips over my land,
    My flat land, my Flanders.

Ay, Marieke, Marieke, the Flemish sky,
Color of the towers of Bruges and Ghent,
Ay, Marieke, Marieke, the Flemish sky
Weeps with me from Bruges to Ghent.

    Without love, warm love,
    The wind blows; it is finished,
    Without love, warm love,
    The sea weeps, already finished.
    Without love, warm love,
    The light flickers; all is finished,
    And the sand whips over my land,
    My flat land, my Flanders.

Ay, Marieke, Marieke, the Flemish sky;
Does it weigh too heavily from Bruges to Ghent,
Ay, Marieke, Marieke, on your twenty years
That I loved so much from Bruges to Ghent?

    Without love, warm love,
    The devil, the black devil, laughs,
    Without love, warm love,
    My heart, my old heart, burns.
    Without love, warm love,
    The summer, the sad summer, dies,
    And the sand whips over my land,
    My flat land, my Flanders.

Ay, Marieke, Marieke, let the time return,
The time of Bruges and Ghent
Ay, Marieke, Marieke, let the time return
When you loved me from Bruges to Ghent.

Ay, Marieke, Marieke, often at evening,
Between the towers of Bruges and Ghent,
Ay, Marieke, Marieke, all the ponds
Open their arms to me from Bruges to Ghent,
From Bruges to Ghent, from Bruges to Ghent.

Angel On My Side

2. In the mornin' I'd wake up and shake my weary head,
   Wonder where I'd been and what I'd said.
   Was I on the River Styx for all eternity?
   Would I drown forever in the sea?
   Why did anyone keep livin', what was there to find?
   Though I wanted just a little peace of mind. *(Chorus)*

3. Never had a flash of lightnin' comin' right at me,
   One day I just know I woke up free.
   The day was breakin', I was livin', I couldn't tell you why,
   First I laughed and then I learned to cry.
   Somethin' in my heart was sayin' you can reach the sky,
   You just gotta live until you die. *(Chorus and 3rd ending)*

Bright Morning Stars

Arranged and Adapted by
Judy Collins

Freely, with expression

Bright morning stars are rising. Bright morning stars are rising. Bright morning stars are rising. Day is breaking in my soul. Oh

Easy Times

Words and Music by
Judy Collins and Stacy Keach, Jr.

Chorus:

Eas - y times come hard for me and oh, my dar - lin', Time a - gain____ to dream____ that you are

Sky Fell

Words and Music by
Judy Collins

Moderately

110

Out Of Control

Words and Music by
Judy Collins

115

Out of con-trol _____ you spin me,

Take me a-gain, your love is win-ning me. I'd fol-low you

an-y-where you say, _____ I fell in love with

you to-day. _____

Shoot First

Words and Music by
Judy Collins

Freely, a cappella
No Chords

"The min - strel boy___ to the war is gone, In the
fa - ther's sword___ he has gird - ed on, And his

1. ranks of death ___ you'll___ find him. His
wild of harp swung___ be - hind him.

2. him."

Quasi march tempo *No chords*
marcato

Verse:

Dm   C   Dm   C   Am   C   Gadd9/A

1. Go get your guns, it's time to play.   Let's hur - ry up, don't waste the day.

You've got - ta shoot first, And ask your ques-tions lat - er.

Shoot first, You've got - ta shoot first. Shoot first,

You got - ta get them be - fore they get you.

Freely, a cappella

No chords

"Land of song," said the war - rior bard, "Though

all the world be - trays_____ thee, One

sword at least_____ thy_____ rights shall guard. One____

poco a poco ritard.

faith - ful harp____ shall praise thee!"

2. My older brother has his own,
It's got a handle made of bone.
He carries it all over town,
Just like on the TV.
My daddy gave my mama one,
Genuine real pearl-handled gun.
She says she's gonna have some fun,
Just like on the TV.

Did you see who got shot last night?
I stayed up to watch him.
They rushed him off to surgery,
Right there on the TV.
Gosh, I hope they catch the guy,
I think they ought to shoot him.
But if they bring him in alive,
He'll be on the TV.   *(Chorus)*

3. I've got to go, it's gettin' late,
I wish I had a real gun.
Then I would never be afraid,
Like some guys on TV.
I'd never use my gun on you,
You'd never have to worry.
You'd be the good guy on my side,
Just like on the TV.

I think when I grow up some day,
I'm gonna be a Green Beret.
I saw them sailing off to war,
Last night on the TV.
My daddy says it's not a game,
We've got to play to win it.
He says I'll have to learn to fight,
Just like on the TV.   *(Chorus and 3rd ending)*

The Moon Is A Harsh Mistress

Jimmy Webb wrote this song, and David Geffen brought it to my attention in 1974. I think it's one of the most evocative songs in our American popular song literature.

Words and Music by
Jimmy Webb

Pretty Polly

Arranged and Adapted by
Judy Collins and Michael Sahl

Moderately slow, with a beat

some pleas-ure to see. _____ She

jumped up be-hind_____ him and a-way they did ride,
Wil-lie, oh Wil-lie, I'm a-feared for my life, Oh

Jumped up be-hind_____ him, a-way they did go,_____
Wil-lie, oh Wil-lie, I'm a-feared for my life,_____ I'm a-

O-ver the moun-tain and the val-ley so low._____
fraid you mean to mur-der me and leave me be-hind."_____

He stabbed her through the heart and her heart blood did flow, _____

He stabbed her__ through the heart__ and her heart blood did flow,

And in-to__ the grave _____ Pret-ty Pol-ly did go. _____

He threw a lit-tle dirt on her and start-ed for home,__

Since You've Asked

This was my first song. Because of that position in my writing, it has always been a particular favorite. It was inspired by many things, including the writings of Leonard Cohen, Joni Mitchell, and the diaries of Anaïs Nin.

Words and Music by
Judy Collins

The Life You Dream

Words and Music by
Judy Collins

Song For Martin

Mart Hoffman was a willowy, lean singer with a sweet, dusty voice.
I first heard him sing "This Land Is Your Land" in the mountains of Colorado.

Words and Music by
Judy Collins

Slowly, with expression

In Rough Rock, Ar - i - zo - na,_____ he lived_____ for man-y years a - lone,_____

A gan-gly kid from Col - o - ra - do who could_____ sing the sweet-est

Don't Say Goodbye Love

Words and Music by
Judy Collins

154

2. Nightmares come, I know I've had one,
   Why can't I be awake, say it's just a dream.
   This is all too real for dreaming,
   Like something in a play, truer than it seems.

   How did your face of love turn to hate?
   Only a moment passed, now it's too late.
   Blind to the truth I have loved,
   Lost for now, I am helpless without you. *(Chorus)*

3. High above the moon is riding,
   Clouds covering her face so she cannot see.
   Tears are falling from my own eyes,
   Hope dying and my heart struggles to be free.

   I want to hide in the past,
   Where I thought that I'd found love at last.
   Love that would suffer my sins,
   Love that would let me begin to live. *(Chorus and 3rd ending)*

Holly Ann (The Weaver Song)

Written for my beloved sister, Holly Ann, under whose fingertips beautiful weavings,
paintings, pottery, jewelry, and the best meals I've ever eaten have emerged.

Words and Music by
Judy Collins

Moderately

158

Granddaddy

Words and Music by
Judy Collins

1. Grand-dad-dy, look at the gyp-sies danc-ing in the fi - re-
2. Can we go down to the rail - road tracks and watch the trains go

light,
by,

Burn - ing so bright - ly.
Shin - ing like sil - ver?

How do they keep them-selves warm on such a night?
I hear the whis - tle, the train is on its way.

When you were young and you sailed up-on the sea.

Wrap me up in your win-ter coat, Wrap me up so tight.

I nev-er will feel the cold. I'll be warm to-night.

1. I'll

2. I'll be safe_____ to-night._____

poco a poco ritard e dim.

3. Granddaddy, tell me the names of all the stars up in the sky,
   Is there a heaven?
   Do you think there is a life after we die?
   Why do some people have all the gold and silver they can spend?
   Others have nothing.
   It isn't fair and I've always wondered why.

   Can I hold the match while you light up your pipe?
   I love the smell of tobacco in the air.
   Tell me again about how it was before I came to be
   In the old country *(To Coda)*

Dream On

Words and Music by
Judy Collins

Moderately

1. Pinch me, dar-lin', I think I'm dream-in', this is too good— to be true.— I've spent my whole life

2. I've spent a lot of years runnin' around, walkin' fast in little towns.
   I had a lot of men offer me love, and I didn't turn all of them down.
   I never knew a man like you, never in my born days.
   If you're a dream, oh, don't let me wake,
   Let me dream on. *(Chorus)*

3. I've never been so close to heaven, never felt so much at home.
   It's like an old-time forties movie where nobody winds up alone.
   I knew somewhere there were dreams comin' true, finally one of them's mine.
   If you're a dream, please let me believe
   That life could be so fine. *(Chorus al Coda)*

Nightingale

Words and Music by
Judy Collins

The Rest Of Your Life

Words and Music by
Judy Collins

3. I on-ly hope you will be hap - py, I want the ver - y best for you. The on-ly prize_____ that's worth the bat - tle_____ Is find - ing love,_____ you know it's true._____

D.S. % al Fine

2. The road we walked was never easy,
   I know I stumbled on the way.
   I thought I knew what I was doing,
   When I was wrong you had to pay.

   I hope by now you can forgive me,
   And take the good I had to give.
   I was too young to be your teacher,
   We learned together how to live. *(Chorus)*

Simple Gifts

Adapted by
Judy Collins

This Is The Day

Words and Music by
Judy Collins and Cynthia McDonald

Trust Your Heart

Words and Music by
Judy Collins

188

made for fools, _____ and

which are wise men's dreams. _____

Trust your heart, _____

poco rit.

mp freely

Trust your heart. _____

ritard. e dim.

R.H.

pp

My Father

This song is not strictly autobiographical—the details had to do with fitting the rhymes into my own emotions. My father never heard the song...he died three weeks after I wrote it.

Words and Music by
Judy Collins

Moderately, in 6, nostalgic

1. My fa-ther al-ways prom-ised us ____ that we would live in France, ____ We'd go boat-ing on the Seine

in time.

Verse 2. All my sisters soon were gone
   to Denver and Cheyenne,
   Marrying their grownup dreams,
   the lilacs and the man.
   I stayed behind the youngest still,
   only danced alone,
   The colors of my father's dreams
   faded without a sigh.

3. And I live in Paris now,
   my children dance and dream
   Hearing the ways of a miner's life
   in words they've never seen.
   I sail my memories of home
   like boats across the Seine,
   And watch the Paris sun
   set in my father's eyes again.

4. My father always promised us
   that we would live in France.
   We'd go boating on the Seine
   and I would learn to dance.
   I sail my memories afar
   like boats across the Seine,
   And watch the Paris sun
   set in my father's eyes again.